The Big Book of Science

Written by David Cullen

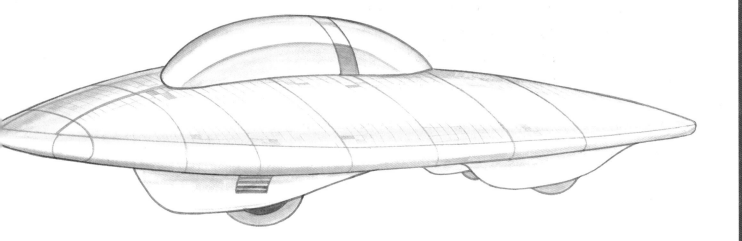

Illustrated by David Leeks

BRIMAX

Contents

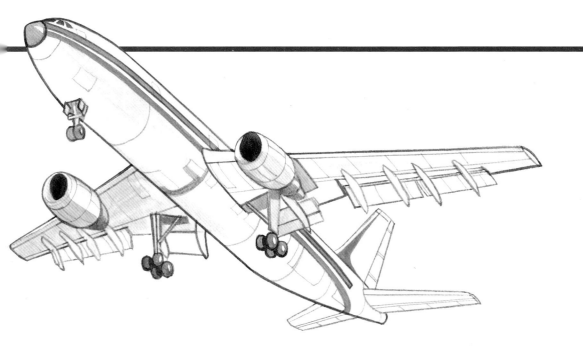

Introduction

Science is everywhere. It is all around us—
at home, in the garden, under the sea, and high
in the sky. Science provides answers to many
puzzling questions, such as why plants need
sunlight, why there are so many colors, how a
rocket can fly, and what makes an ice cube melt.

This book will show you just how much fun
learning about science can be. Each topic is
simply explained and supported by bright
illustrations, amazing facts, and interesting
experiments to do at home.

Get an
adult to
help you!

Look out for this sign on the
page. It will tell you that you
will need the help of an
adult and it will warn you
about anything dangerous.

Water

You can find water in a great many places. It comes out of our taps, flows past in rivers, makes huge waves in the sea, and it is even in the air that you breathe.

Water cycle

Water falls as rain onto the ground where it collects together to form streams and rivers, which flow towards the sea. Here, the water evaporates (becomes a gas) into the air, ready to fall as rain again. This is known as the water cycle.

Flooding

When there has been a lot of rain, rivers may overflow and flood surrounding areas, causing a lot of damage.

Water always flows downhill, in streams and rivers.

Tap water

Tap water has to be processed and filtered before it is ready for us to drink.

Did you know?

There is a lot of water in the world. In fact, nearly two-thirds of the Earth's surface is covered in water!

Sometimes, water collects into lakes.

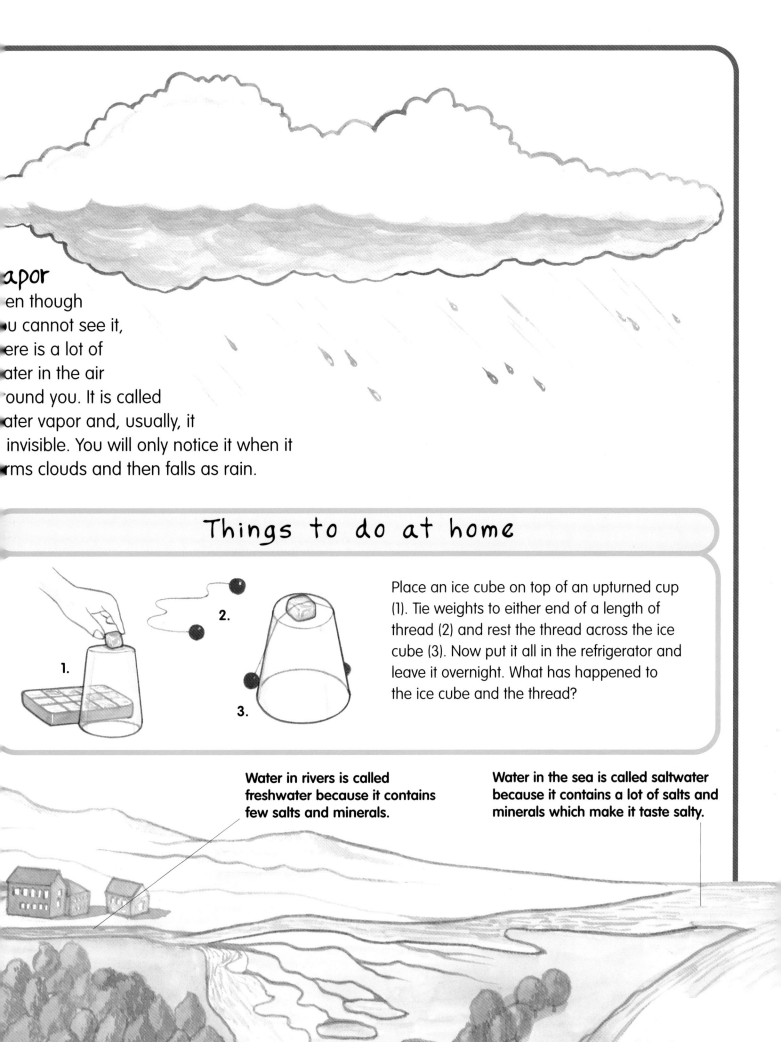

...apor

...en though
...u cannot see it,
...ere is a lot of
...ater in the air
...ound you. It is called
...ater vapor and, usually, it
...invisible. You will only notice it when it
...rms clouds and then falls as rain.

Things to do at home

1.

2.

3.

Place an ice cube on top of an upturned cup (1). Tie weights to either end of a length of thread (2) and rest the thread across the ice cube (3). Now put it all in the refrigerator and leave it overnight. What has happened to the ice cube and the thread?

Water in rivers is called freshwater because it contains few salts and minerals.

Water in the sea is called saltwater because it contains a lot of salts and minerals which make it taste salty.

Ice

Normally, water is runny stuff which we call a liquid. However, if it gets very cold, the tiny particles which make up water join together to form ice. This is known as a solid. When water turns into a solid, it is known as freezing.

North Pole

South Pole

Floating ice

Ice actually weighs less than water. This is why ice cubes float in a drink and icebergs float in the sea.

Poles

At the top and bottom of our planet are cold areas called the North and South Poles. These chilly regions are covered with thick layers of ic and snow.

About four-fifths of an iceberg sits below the water.

Did you know?

In the winter, water in outdoor pipes can freeze. Because water expands (gets bigger) when it freezes, it can burst the pipes!

Icebergs

Icebergs are large, floating pieces of ice. Some of them can be as big as a whole country! They break away from the ice sheets at the North and South Poles and drift across the sea. They can be dangerous, and some have even sunk ships.

Icicles

Have you ever looked out of your window on a cold winter's day and seen icicles hanging from your roof? These have been made by water dripping off the roof and freezing. This forms the long, hanging spikes of ice we call icicles.

Snow

Snowflakes are actually tiny pieces of frozen water. They may all look the same when they fall, but each snowflake is completely different from any other. You can squash snowflakes together to make snowballs and snow people.

Things to do at home

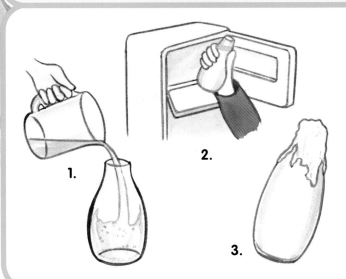

Fill up a plastic bottle with water and mark the water level (1). Place the bottle in the freezer (2) and leave it over night. Once the water in the bottle has frozen, take the bottle out of the freezer and note the level of the ice (3). Is the level of the ice higher or lower than the level of the water?

Steam

The air around you and the exhaust fumes from a car are examples of gases. Water can become a gas if it is heated enough and starts to bubble. This is called boiling. When water boils, it turns into a gas called steam.

Boiling water

You can see water turn into steam when an adult boils it in a kettle. Sometimes, the steam makes a whistling sound as it comes out of the kettle.

The tallest geysers can reach a heig of 1,500 feet (450 meters)

Geysers

These tall jets of steam and hot water that shoot naturally out of the ground are not very different from a kettle. Water is heated by hot rocks under the ground. When the water gets hot enough, it shoots up high above the surface.

Steam power

If steam collects in a small space it can create a large pushing force. The first trains used steam to push them along tracks.

Did you know?

Scientists have found tiny amounts of water on the Moon. They have also found evidence that water used to flow on the surface of Mars.

Condensation

You can see steam turn back into water when it cools down on a cold window. It forms small drops of water on the glass. These drops are called condensation.

Things to do at home

Fill two saucers with the same amount of water. Place one on a sunny window ledge and the other in a refrigerator. Over the next couple of days, mark the level of water in each saucer. Which puddle of water disappears the quickest?

Mixing and separating

Very few things are pure. Instead, they may be a mixture of different chemicals and substances. Here are some mixtures you might come across every day, as well as the different methods scientists use to separate some mixtures.

Rivers

Rivers do not just contain water. They also carry a mixture of dirt and small stones which the water picks up as it flows over the ground. Fast-flowing rivers can pick up a lot of dirt and stones, which, over many years, may carve out long valleys called gorges.

Pure water?

Even though it looks pure, the water from your tap has many minerals and chemicals mixed into it which make it safe to drir

In towns, some rivers contain a lot of rubbish and pollution.

Some factories release chemicals into rivers.

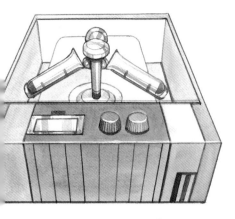

pinning around

ne method that scientists use
separate a mixture is to
in it around very fast in a
vice called a centrifuge.
the mixture spins
ound, the heavier
bstances in the
xture settle to
e bottom,
aving the
hter ones
the top.

Mix together some sand, soil,
sticks, and stones in a jug of
water (1). Then pour the mixture
through a sieve (2). What
has been left behind in
the sieve and how clear
is the water? Now pour
the remaining mixture
through some filter paper
(3). Does the water look
any clearer than before it
was filtered?

1.

2.

3.

Did you know?

The Grand Canyon
in Arizona, USA
was carved by the
Colorado river.
The canyon itself
measures over one
mile (1.6 kilometers)
from top to bottom.

Slicks and spills

Not everything mixes together. You might have seen how oil floats on water or how some dirt cannot be rinsed away. Sometimes you need to use another substance, like soap, to make things mix.

Soap

Oil and water do not mix. As a result, oily dirt cannot be rinsed off just by using water. Instead, you need to use soap as well. Soap binds the dirt to the water and allows it to be washed away from your skin.

Sometimes, special chemicals are sprayed onto an oil spill. These break up the spill and stop it from causing a lot of damage.

Oil spills

Oil spills can be very dangerous. On the land, the oil can poison the soil and get into rivers. At sea, the oil floats on top of the water and it can damage sea plants and animals. There are many ways of cleaning up an oil spill at sea. These include using barriers to keep the spill in one place or special machines to skim the oil off the surface.

Did you know?

The largest oil slick in the world took place in the Gulf of Mexico in 1979 when 166 million US gallons (630 million liters) of oil spilled out of an oil well.

Oil spills at sea can be very big because the largest supertankers can carry millions of gallons of oil.

Paint

Some paints are not actually proper mixtures. Instead, they are made up of tiny drops of oil that are scattered in water. These paints are called emulsions.

Things to do at home

1.

Carefully pour some syrup, water, and oil into a tall glass (1). Now look at the liquids in the glass (2). Have they mixed together, or are they sitting in separate layers?

2.

Oil

Water

Syrup

Floating and sinking

Have you ever wondered why a small pebble sinks and a huge ship floats? Even though the pebble is small, it actually weighs more than the same volume of water, so it sinks. The huge ship actually weighs less than the same volume of water, so it floats.

Can you float?

Inside your body there are lots of air spaces. These make you light enough to float in water, even without the use of an inflatable ring.

Getting heavy

The more you load onto a boat, the heavier it gets and the lower it sinks in the water. On the sides of many boats are marks called the Plimsoll line. These show the safe levels at which the boat should float when it is empty and when it is fully loaded.

Did you know?

The biggest ships in the world are huge supertankers which can be as long as four soccer pitches!

Surface tension

Some insects appear to float on the water's surface. In fact, they are using a force known as surface tension. This is the force which binds the tiny particles of water together at the surface and which stops the insects from sinking.

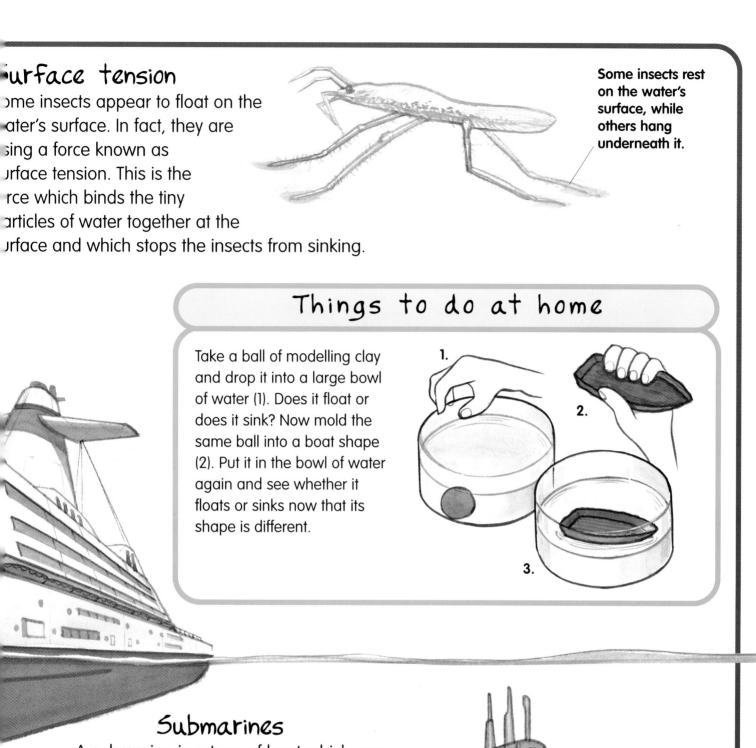

Some insects rest on the water's surface, while others hang underneath it.

Things to do at home

Take a ball of modelling clay and drop it into a large bowl of water (1). Does it float or does it sink? Now mold the same ball into a boat shape (2). Put it in the bowl of water again and see whether it floats or sinks now that its shape is different.

1.
2.
3.

Submarines

A submarine is a type of boat which can go underwater. Special chambers inside the submarine are filled with water to make the submarine heavier so that it can dive under the water. In order to surface, these chambers are filled with air to make the submarine lighter.

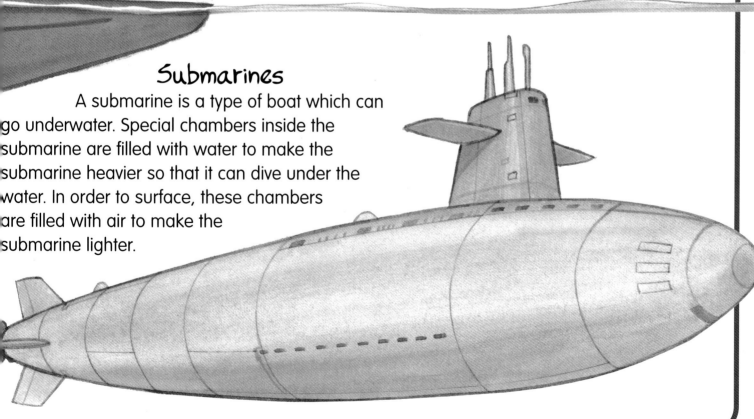

Heating things up

Heat is very useful when it comes to changing things. Heat can change ice into water and water into steam. We use heat to cook our food and to shape metals. In nature, heat can make beautiful stones and it can even melt solid rock!

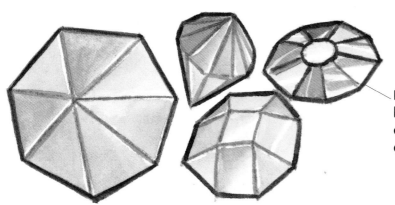

Diamonds are so hard that they can only be cut using other diamonds.

Diamonds

Diamonds are made from carbon, the same chemical that makes black coal. But these rocks have been heated and crushed to turn them into sparkling gems.

Bread

Before bread is baked, it is a mushy, squishy substance called dough. Heating the dough in an oven changes it into the crusty bread which we eat.

Did you know?

The biggest loaf of bread ever baked was nearly 10 feet (3 meters) long and weighed over 1.5 tons!

Steel

When metals are heated enough, they melt. This lets us bend and shape the metals into useful objects, such as metal girders for buildings, body parts for cars and planes, or tools.

Squeeze the juice from a lemon into a glass (1). Using the juice, paint a picture onto a plain piece of paper (2). Before long, the lemon juice will dry and your picture will disappear. Now ask an adult to place the paper in a warm oven (3). After a few minutes, ask an adult to take the paper out. What has happened to the lemon juice? Is your picture still invisible?

1.

2.

3.

Get an adult to help you!

4.

The liquid rock that flows over the ground is called lava.

Volcano

Deep inside the Earth huge forces heat, squash, and squeeze rocks so much that they melt. Sometimes, this liquid rock erupts from the ground, creating volcanoes.

Solar power

The Sun is an important source of energy. It warms our planet, gives us light, helps plants to live, and can even b used to make electricity to power calculators, cars, and some homes!

The Sun

The Sun is an enormous ball of hot burning gas. Even though it is 96 million miles (154 million kilometers) away from the Earth, its powerful rays can still harm you!

Solar car

Some cars run on power from the Sun instead of normal fuel. These cars have special solar cells, which change sunlight into electricity.

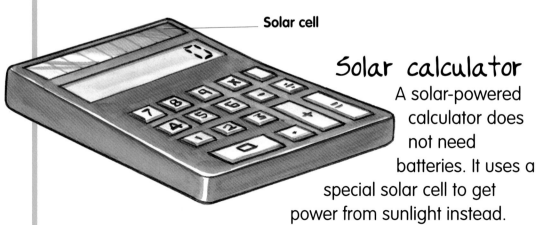

Solar cell

Solar calculator

A solar-powered calculator does not need batteries. It uses a special solar cell to get power from sunlight instead.

Did you know?

Every year, a race is held in Australia especially for solar-powered cars. These cars drive for thousands of miles, powered only by the Sun.

Things to do at home

Thermometer

You can see the difference the Sun can make to the temperature by using a thermometer. Place one thermometer in a sunny area and another in the shade (1). After a couple of minutes, make a note of the temperatures on the thermometers (2). Which temperature is higher?

2.

1.

Sun protection

When out on a sunny day, it is important to be protected from the Sun's rays. Wear a hat, loose clothing, and plenty of sun screen.

Make sure that you rub in sun screen, even if you are wearing clothes!

Solar house

People in sunny countries can fit solar panels to the roofs of their houses to provide power and heat.

Structures

Every day, you use a variety of buildings and structures, which must be made just the right shape and from the right materials to best suit their particular purpose. They could be homes to live in, offices to work in, places to have fun in, or routes to get from one place to another.

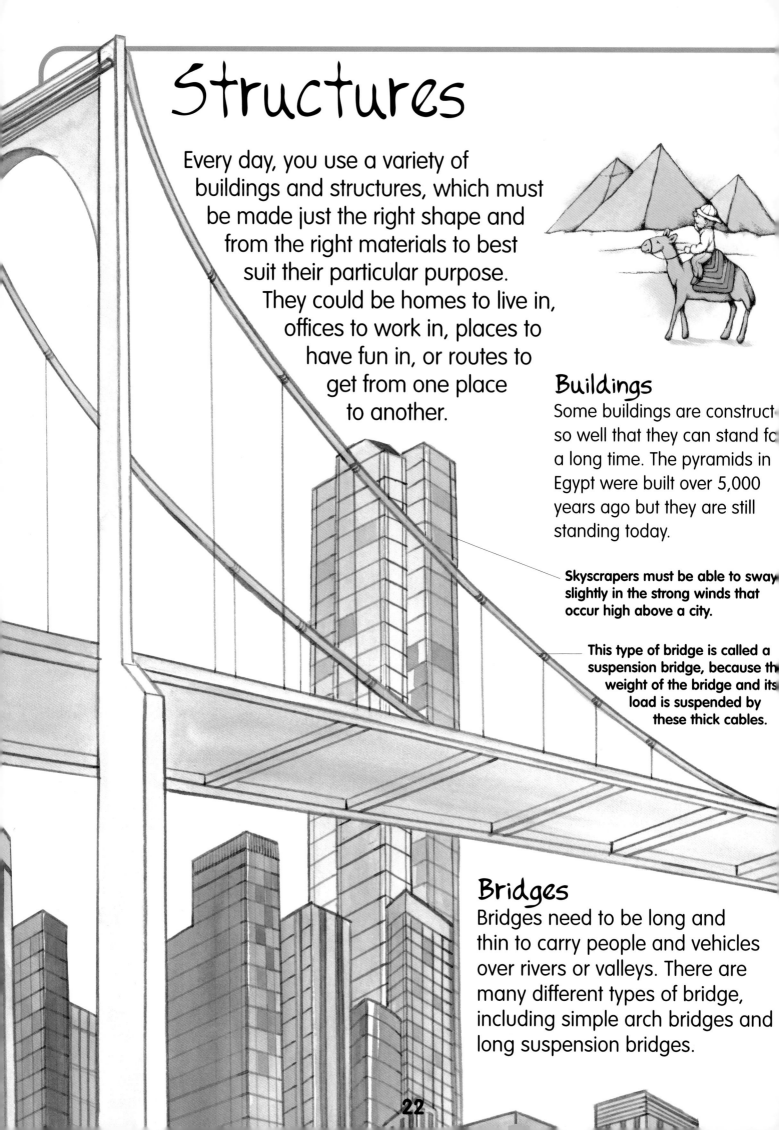

Buildings
Some buildings are construct so well that they can stand fc a long time. The pyramids in Egypt were built over 5,000 years ago but they are still standing today.

Skyscrapers must be able to sway slightly in the strong winds that occur high above a city.

This type of bridge is called a suspension bridge, because th weight of the bridge and its load is suspended by these thick cables.

Bridges
Bridges need to be long and thin to carry people and vehicles over rivers or valleys. There are many different types of bridge, including simple arch bridges and long suspension bridges.

Animal structures

Animals also build things. Beavers build dams and lodges and birds make nests. Spiders build large webs from a strong silk which they produce in their bodies. A single strand of spider's silk is stronger than a strand of steel of the same thickness.

Things to do at home

1.

2.

3.

Test the strength of a cardboard tube. First stand a pair of cardboard tubes on their ends and balance a book on top of them (1). Now add more books (2), and see how many the tubes can support before collapsing. Now repeat the test, but this time with the tubes on their sides (3). Can they support more or less books this time?

Did you know?

The longest bridges have to take the curved shape of the Earth into account when they are being built.

Light and shade

On a sunny day, everywhere appears to be bright. However, if you look carefully, you will see some dark patches in areas where the light cannot reach. These dark areas are known as shadows.

Shade safety
Sitting in the shade will make you feel cooler on a sunny day. However, the Sun's rays can still harm you, and you will need to wear sun screen

Moving sun
Throughout the day, the Sun appears to move across the sky. As the Sun moves, so do any shadows. People use the moving Sun and shadows to tell the time and direction.

Shadows
A shadow is caused when an object, such as your body or a building, blocks the light rays' path, leaving a darker, shaded area. When there is more than one light source or more than one object, you might see many shadows.

Did you know?
The ancient Babylonians used shadow clocks to tell the time over 4,000 years ago!

1.

2.

Build your own shadow clock. First push a long stick into the ground and mark the point where its shadow falls (1). Then, one hour later, mark the point on the ground where the shadow has moved to. Do this for several hours until you have built up a number of points (2). See how accurately your shadow clock keeps time.

Never look directly at the Sun!

tars

e Sun isn't the only ight object in the sky. n a clear night, you n see the bright surface of e Moon as well as thousands stars. These stars are very e the Sun, but they are much rther away.

See if you can make shadow shapes using your hands.

Eclipses

Sometimes the Moon moves in front of the Sun, blocking out its light and causing an eclipse. Even though it is ark, you must never look at an eclipse ithout wearing special glasses.

Color

Animals and people use colors in lots of different ways. Colors can make things bright and cheerful, they can warn of danger, or they can be used to hide from watchful eyes.

Rainbows

Sunlight is a mixture of lo of different colors of light. You c see these colors when a rainbow is formed. This is caused by raindrops scattering the sunlight and splitting it up into a band of many colors.

Did you know?

The human eye can detect up to 10 million different colors, from red to violet. How many colors can you name?

Animal colors

There are many colorful animals. Some, such as the beautiful peacock use color to attract a mate. Others, such as the striped tiger, use it to he them hide from other animals.

The colors of a rainbow are red, orange, yellow, green, blue, indigo, and violet.

Primary colors

You can create all the colors of the rainbow by mixing together just three colors, called primary colors. Artists use the primary colors red, blue, and yellow to get all the colors they need.

Changing light

Light can be changed when it passes through objects. Some objects bend light. This is called refraction. Other objects can change the color of light.

Stained glass changes the color of light.

Things to do at home

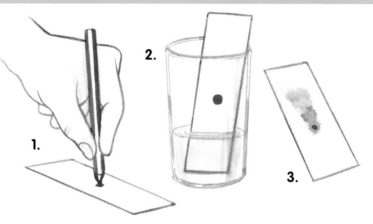

1.

2.

3.

Take a water-based marker or some ink and draw a blob of color onto a strip of filter paper (1). Then place the strip of filter paper into a glass with a small amount of water in the bottom (2). Leave the filter paper for a few minutes and then take it out and look at the blob of color (3). What has happened to the color? Has it stayed the same?

Plants and light

Plants like a bright sunny day. Sunshine is very important to plants. They use it to produce the energy they need to stay alive and to keep growing. Without any sunshine, plants would wither away and die.

Sunflowers grow very tall to get above other plants and reach the sunlight.

Houseplants

Plants always grow towards sunlight. If you have some plant in your home, you must turn them around every so often, so that they grow evenly.

Green leaves

Have you ever wondered why plants are green? This green color in plants is a special substance called chlorophyll. This substance helps the plants to absorb sunlight.

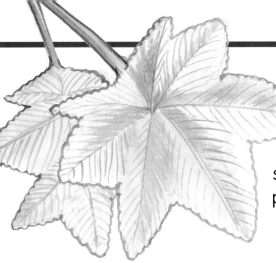

Hungry plants

Plants need sunlight because it helps them to produce energy, which they need to live and grow. When you eat plant food, such as a salad or some bread, you release the energy that the plant has produced. This helps you to live and grow as well.

Things to do at home

Cut out a shape from a piece of card (1). Soak some cotton wool in water and place it in a tray. Then scatter some cress seeds over the cotton wool (2). Cover the seeds with the card and leave the tray on a window ledge for a few days (3). Then take off the card and look at the cress (4). How well have the seeds grown that were in the shade and how well have the seeds grown that were in the light?

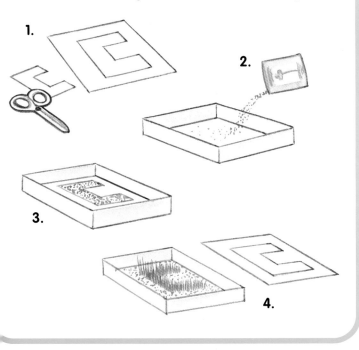

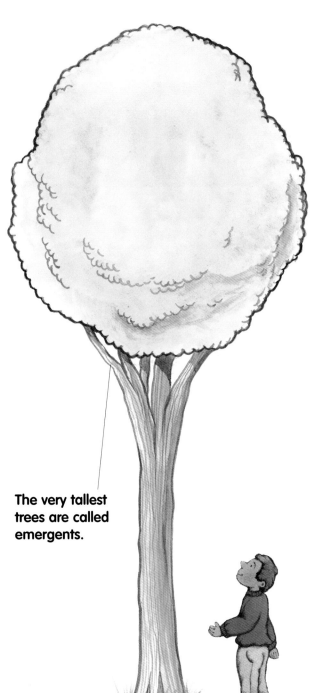

The very tallest trees are called emergents.

Did you know?

Scientists have found plants and animals that don't need sunlight at all. These creatures live on the sea bed, near underwater volcanoes which supply them with food to live.

Tall trees

In thick forests, some trees grow very tall indeed so that their leaves can reach above the other trees and find the sunlight.

29

Plants and water

As well as sunlight, plants need lots of water to stay healthy. However, they don't drink water through a mouth like you do. Instead, they draw water up from the ground using their roots.

Floating plants

Not all plants grow in the same way. Some, such as water lilies, even grow on water. Their leaves and flowers float on the surface, while their stems hang in the water below. Their roots attach the plant to the bottom of the pond and suck up water.

These water lilies have large, flat leaves which help them to float on water.

Thirsty plants

Plant stems and roots have narrow tubes inside them, just like lots of little drinking straws. Water is drawn up these tubes and into the plant.

The roots of a plant grow beneath the soil to find water and food.

Things to do at home

Mix some food coloring in with a glass of water (1). Then stand some white flowers in the glass of colored water (2). After a couple of days, have a look at the flowers. Are they still the same color?

1.

2.

3.

Did you know?

The tallest flower in the world is a type of rhododendron which can grow to a height of 65 feet (20 meters)!

The prickles on a cactus stop animals from reaching the water inside the cactus' stem.

esert plants

me plants, such as cacti, have
live in dry places where it
rdly ever rains. These
ints survive by storing
ge amounts of water
their thick stems.

Sounds

Sounds are actually waves in the air. When you make a sound, you cause the tiny particles that make up the air to shake, or vibrate. These vibrations, called sound waves, travel through the air until they reach an ear and the sound is heard.

Ear bones

On the telephone

Telephones convert the sounds you make into special signals. These signals are sent to other telephones which convert them back into sounds so that other people can hear what you are saying.

Small bones

Inside your ear are three of the smallest bones in your body. These tiny bones help you to hear sounds. They ar called the hammer, anvil, ar stirrup bones.

Sounds made by whales can be heard many miles away.

Underwater sounds

Sounds travel very well underwater. Many fish and sea mammals, such as whales and dolphins, use sounds to find things and to communicate with each other.

Things to do at home

Ask an adult to pierce a small hole in the bottom of two plastic cups. Then take a long piece of string and push each end of the string through these holes and tie a knot to hold it there (1). Then you and a friend each take a cup and stand apart so that the string is tight (2). Talk into one of the cups and see if your friend can hear what you are saying.

1.

Get an adult to help you!

2.

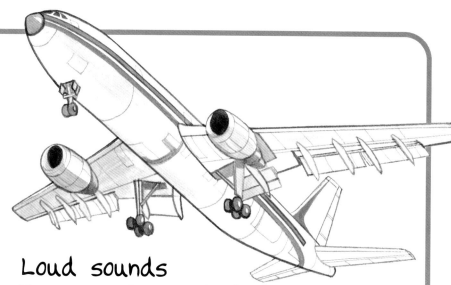

Loud sounds

Your ears can hear very loud noises, such as the roar of a jet plane taking off. However, too many loud noises can damage your hearing, so be careful.

Quiet sounds

Your ears are so sensitive that they can also hear very faint sounds, including the quiet rustling of leaves in a breeze.

Did you know?

The telephone was invented by Alexander Graham Bell in 1876. The first words said on a telephone were "Mr. Watson, come here, I want you."

Magnets

A magnet is an object that has the ability to attract some metals, such as iron. Magnets can also attract or push away other magnets. This can make them very useful in a junkyard or on a high-speed train.

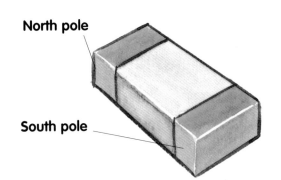

North pole

South pole

Opposites attract

A magnet has two ends, called the north pole and the south pole. If two magnets have the same poles put near each other, they will push away. But if one of the magnets is turned over, the two different poles will attract each other.

Finding your way

The Earth acts like a huge magnet. It also has two magnetic poles, called the North Pole and the South Pole. A compass uses the Earth's magnetism to show you the right direction. It will always point north.

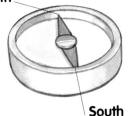

North

South

Magnet crane

In a junkyard, huge cranes with enormous magnets on the end are used to lift tons of metal. These special magnets also use electricity, so they can be turned on and off. This means that they can pick up the metal and then drop it.

Magnetic train

A maglev train (short for magnetic levitation) uses magnets that push against each other to float above the tracks. Because the train does not touch the tracks, it can zoom along more smoothly and much faster than normal trains.

Things to do at home

Tape a bar magnet to the top of a toy car (1). Then use another bar magnet to push the car along, making sure that two poles which are the same are near each other (2). Can you move the magnet you are holding and steer your car through a course (3)?

1.

2.

3.

Did you know?

The Earth's magnetic poles do not stay still. They wobble about and, every 10 million years, they swap over and the North Pole becomes the South Pole.

NORTH POLE

SOUTH POLE

Electricity

Electricity is a form of power that you use every day. It warms your home and powers your television. Electricity also occurs naturally. It can produce a brilliant flash of lightning or make your hair stand on end.

Static

You can make your own form of natural electricity, called static electricity. Next time you pull off a woollen sweater, you might hear a crackling sound. That sound is made by small sparks of static electricity.

Did you know?

A flash of lightning can heat the air up to 54,000°F (30,000°C) — that is hotter than the surface of the Sun!

A bolt of lightning measures about 2 inches (5 centimeters) across.

Lightning

Lightning is a powerful flash of electricity between storm clouds and the ground. When lightning flashes, it heats up the air and causes loud bursts of thunder. There are about 6,000 lightning flashes around the world every single minute.

WARNING! Electricity is very DANGEROUS!

Things to do at home

Static electricity can act like a magnet and attract certain objects. Rub a balloon against a woollen sweater to build up a static charge (1). Then see if your balloon will stick to a wall (2). You can also try to pick up small pieces of paper. Now try putting the charged balloon next to your hair and see what happens (3).

Personal stereo

Games machine

Television

In your home

Electricity flows into your home, along cables, to power the lights, the oven, and the television. Other sources of electricity are batteries. These power cells can supply small amounts of electricity to objects such as personal stereos, games machines, and wristwatches.

Rough and smooth

When things rub together, it creates a force called friction. This force can be a problem, especially when it comes to moving objects. But it can also be very helpful, if you want to stop or stick to the road.

Tires on cross-country bicycles have a deep tread so that they can get lots of grip in muddy conditions.

Gripping

Friction can be useful when it comes to getting a grip on the road. Tires on a bicycle or a car have a pattern, called the tread. This tread increases the friction between the tire and the road and stops you from sliding around.

Rubbing

Have you ever rubbed yourself to get warm? That's friction between your hands and your body creating heat.

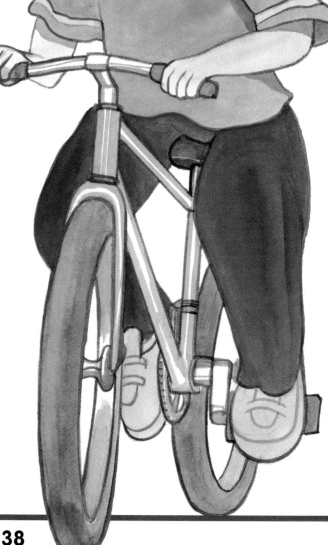

Things to do at home

This project lets you test different levels of friction. Take a hardback book and place a coin at one end (1). Tilt the book until the coin starts to slide down (2). Now place a sheet of sandpaper over the book and repeat the test (3). How much do you have to tilt the book before the coin starts to move this time?

1.

2.

3.

Gliding

Ice skates work by melting the ice directly underneath them. This thin layer of water reduces the friction between the skate and the ice and helps you to glide around easily.

Did you know?

In dry weather, racing cars use special tires without any tread. If they used tires with a tread, the car would go slower and it would lose the race.

Oil is used to make things run smoothly in engines.

Smoothing

Engines and machines need special substances to reduce friction and to make them run smoothly. These special substances are called lubricants.

Stopping and going

People have invented many different ways of reducing friction, including wheels and tracks. Stopping can be very important as well, and there are many ways of slowing something down, including brakes and parachutes.

The wheel

The wheel is one of the oldest and simplest ways of overcoming friction. Instead of dragging along the ground, a wheel rolls around, reducing friction, and making movement easier.

Tracks

Trains use special wheels that run on tracks. These let the train move along at high speeds without the need for steerin

Hovercraft

A hovercraft actually floats above the ground. Huge propellers blow air under the hovercraft, creating a cushion of air. Th hovercraft can then move along with very little friction between itself and the ground.

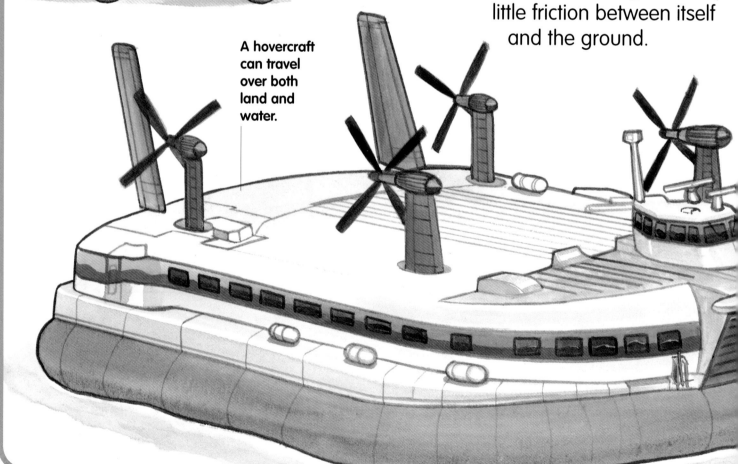

A hovercraft can travel over both land and water.

Did you know?

The first parachute jump was made by a Frenchman called André-Jacques Garnerin in 1797. He jumped out of a hot-air balloon and glided safely down to earth, unhurt.

Bicycle brakes work by pinching the wheel rim.

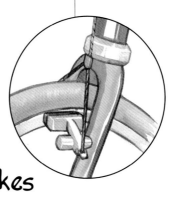

Parachutes

Parachutes work by trapping air beneath them to slow a person down as they fall. Parachutes are also used to slow down dragsters, jet planes, and the Space Shuttle.

Brakes

Friction is very important in stopping vehicles. The brakes on a car and a bicycle work by rubbing up against the wheels as they spin round. This increases the friction, makes it harder for the wheels to spin, and slows the vehicle down.

Things to do at home

You can make your own hovercraft with this simple project. Ask an adult to cut the top off a plastic drinks bottle, as shown here (1). Then blow up a balloon (2). While pinching the neck of the balloon, stretch the end of the balloon over the top of the bottle (3). Now let go of the balloon, and see how easily you can push your hovercraft about.

Get an adult to help you!

1.

2.

3.

Jets and rockets

Jet engines have been used on aircraft for over 70 years. They can push planes to greater speeds and at greater heights than propeller engines. To reach space, however, requires a really powerful engine, called a rocket.

Rocket power

Rockets, such as the Space Shuttle, work by burning fuel with a gas called oxygen. The result is a powerful blast of hot gases which pushes the rocket forward at high speed.

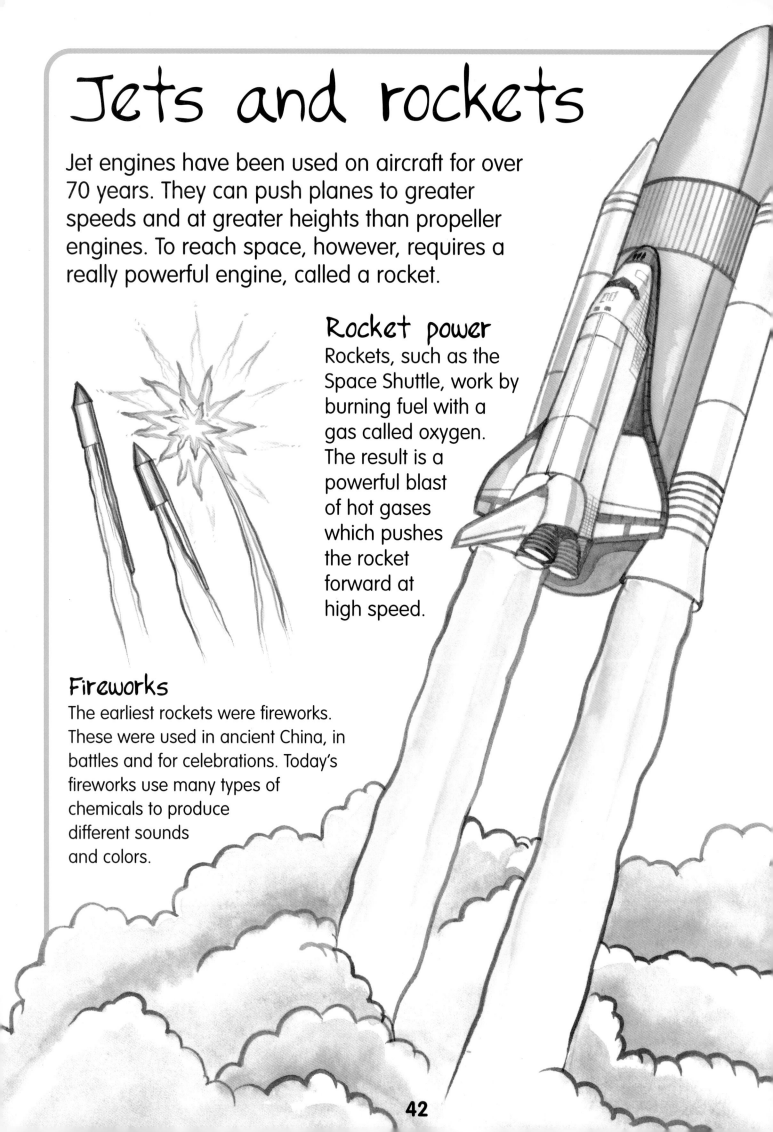

Fireworks

The earliest rockets were fireworks. These were used in ancient China, in battles and for celebrations. Today's fireworks use many types of chemicals to produce different sounds and colors.

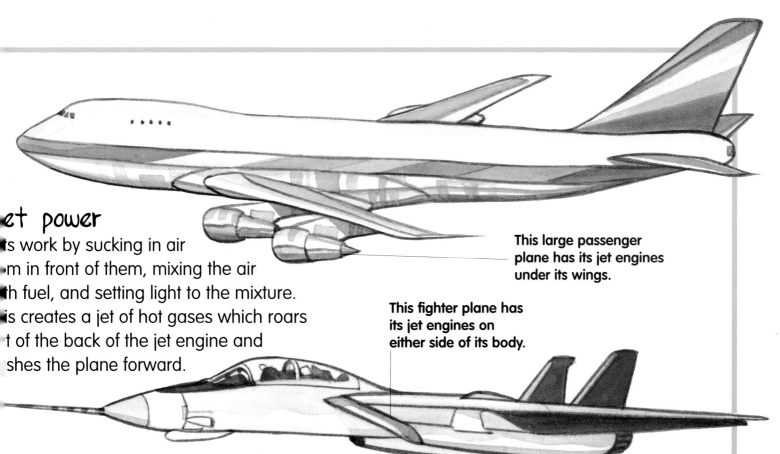

This large passenger plane has its jet engines under its wings.

This fighter plane has its jet engines on either side of its body.

et power

s work by sucking in air
m in front of them, mixing the air
th fuel, and setting light to the mixture.
s creates a jet of hot gases which roars
t of the back of the jet engine and
shes the plane forward.

Things to do at home

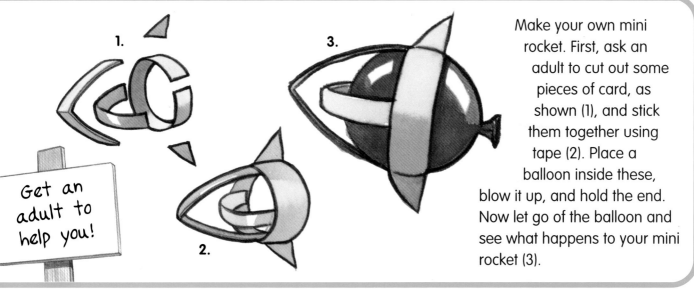

1.

2.

3.

Get an adult to help you!

Make your own mini rocket. First, ask an adult to cut out some pieces of card, as shown (1), and stick them together using tape (2). Place a balloon inside these, blow it up, and hold the end. Now let go of the balloon and see what happens to your mini rocket (3).

Did you know?

The biggest rockets ever built were over 350 feet (110 meters) tall. These were the Saturn V rockets that carried people to the Moon.

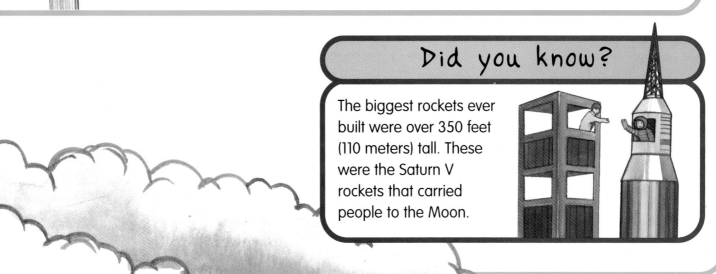

The weather

What is the weather like outside your window today? The type of weather you have can depend on a great many things, such as the time of year, where you live, and even how much pollution there is in the air.

Sun

Rain

Snow

Wind

Extreme weather
Sometimes, the weather can become extremely violent. In some parts of the world, there are huge storms called hurricanes a cyclones. Tornadoes are powerful twisting columns of air which move over the ground. When a tornado occurs at sea, it is called a water spout.

Types of weather
Different parts of the world have different types of weather. Some places might see sunshine, rain, wind, and snow throughout the year. People who live in warmer countries that are near to the Earth's equator, might not see snow at all.

Rain

Cloud

Sun

Weather forecasting

Some scientists specialize in finding out what the weather will be like. They are called meteorologists and they use satellites and special equipment to see what weather might be heading your way.

Things to do at home

Tissue paper

Writing paper

Thin card

Thick card

Get an adult to help you!

Tornadoes are also called twisters because of their swirling funnels of air.

1.

2.

3.

Make your own weather station to record the weather. First, make a wind gauge by tying different weights of paper and card to a stick (1). A strong wind will blow the heavier bits of card. Next, ask an adult to cut the top off a plastic drinks bottle. Then put the top back in the bottle upside down to make a rain collector (2). Finally, use a thermometer to record the temperature (3).

Did you know?

The fastest wind speed recorded was at Mount Washington, USA, on April 12th, 1934. It was 231 mph (397 km/h).

Science words

Boiling
A liquid turns into a gas when the temperature rises to a particular point. Water becomes steam when it reaches boiling point.

Centrifuge
This is a spinning device which scientists use to separate different substances.

Chlorophyll
Plants are green because of chlorophyll. This special substance is found in leaves and helps to convert sunlight and nutrients into energy.

Freezing
A liquid turns into a solid when the temperature drops below a certain point. Water freezes into ice when it gets very cold.

Friction
This is a force that is caused by two objects rubbing against each other. Rough objects can cause a lot of friction, while smooth objects create little friction. Friction can make object difficult to move.

Gases
These are substances that can expand to fill any container. Air is an example of a gas.

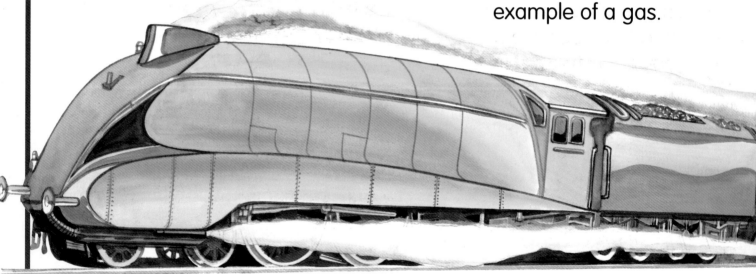

Condensing
A gas turns into a liquid or solid when the temperature falls below a certain point. Steam condenses into water if it cools down or when it touches a cool surface, such as a window.

Jet engines
Jet engines suck in air from in front o them and burn it with fuel. This creates a jet of hot gases which blow out of the back of the engine and pushes the vehicle forward.